'81 0 5 6 2 7

DATE DUE			

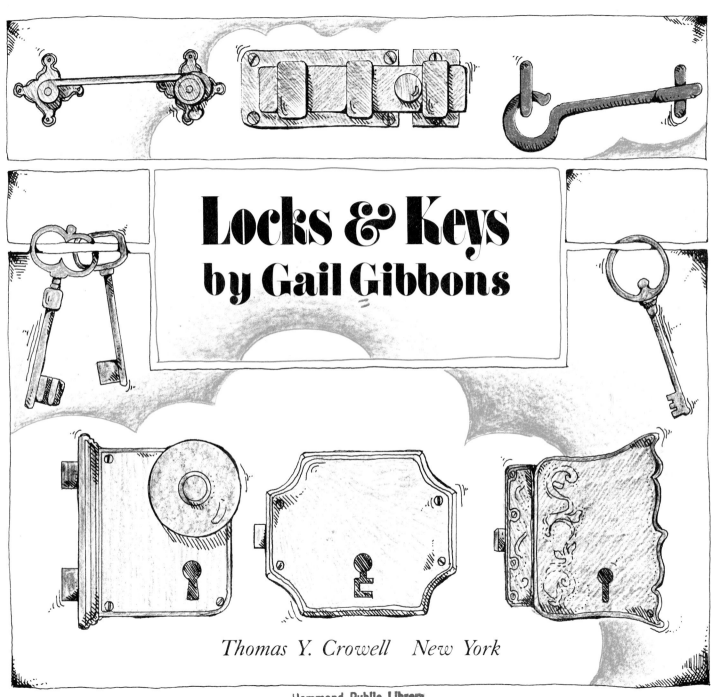

Locks & Keys
by Gail Gibbons

Thomas Y. Crowell   New York

For Royce Ancliffe

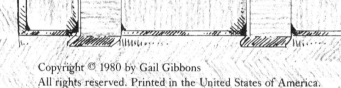

Copyright © 1980 by Gail Gibbons
All rights reserved. Printed in the United States of America.

Library of Congress Cataloging in Publication Data
Gibbons, Gail. Locks & keys.
   SUMMARY: Traces the history of locks and keys from
ancient times to the present, describing the develop-
ment of increasingly complex and pick-proof locks and
how they work.
   1. Locks and keys—Juvenile literature. [1. Locks
and keys] I. Title.
TS521.G5   1980   683'.32   79-7825
ISBN 0-690-04058-X   ISBN 0-690-04059-8 lib. bdg.
1 2 3 4 5 6 7 8 9 10
First Edition

ALSO BY GAIL GIBBONS

Clocks and How They Go

From the beginning, people wanted to protect what they had from thieves and prowling animals. A caveman could roll a boulder in front of his cave opening to keep his animal skins and food from being taken when he wasn't at home. But this wasn't always safe enough.

   For thousands of years, nothing changed very much.
Then Egyptians made the first doors.
   People tried to keep thieves from opening their doors.
They stretched a rope between two knobs, one on the
door and the other on the doorpost. They tied the ends
together in a difficult knot, sealed the knot in wax or clay,
and cast a spell on it.

But many robbers didn't care about the spell. They broke the seal and undid the knot, or just cut the rope with a knife. People soon saw that their idea wasn't a very good one.

They tried latches and sliding bolts. The latch or bolt
stretched across the door to the doorpost to keep the door
from being opened.

Latches and bolts were good for keeping the door
locked from the inside. But a latch or bolt on the outside
could be opened by anyone. People could not leave their
homes and lock their doors behind them.

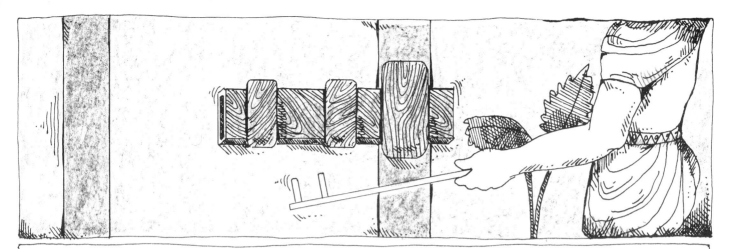

About 4,000 years ago, the first mechanical lock, a lock with moving parts inside, was made in Egypt. This first mechanical lock was opened by using a key. Now you could lock your door on the outside, and no one without a key could open it.

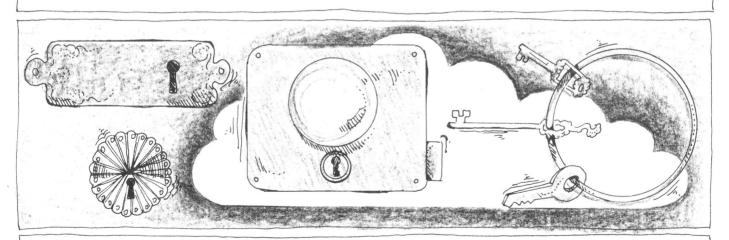

It was the beginning of locks and keys…

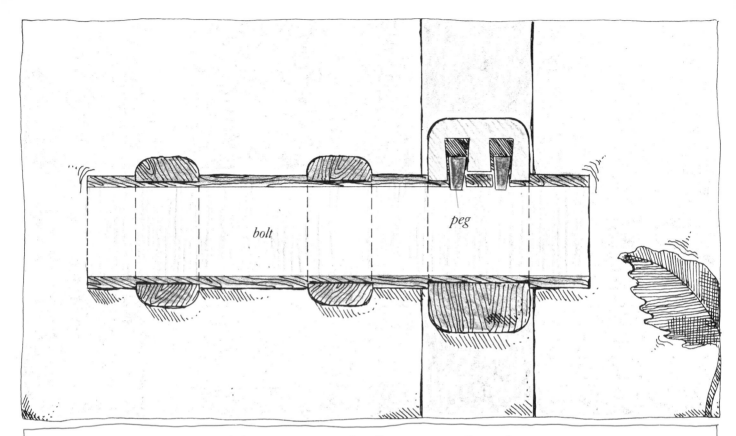

The first lock and key was made from wood and was very big. The main part of the lock was a wooden block attached to the doorpost. The other part was a hollow bolt that rested loosely in brackets fixed to the door. Inside the block were movable wooden pegs. The bolt had small holes near one end. When the bolt was slid over, the pegs in the lock dropped into the holes of the bolt to hold it in place and lock the door.

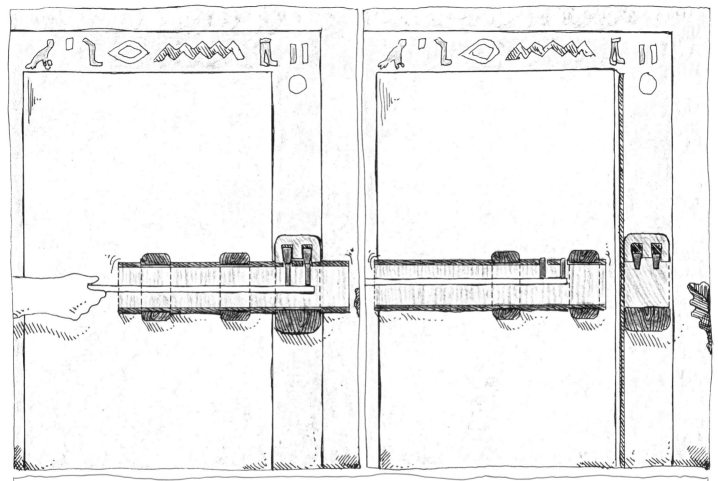

To unlock the door, the key was needed. The key, too, had pegs on one end. It was about three feet long and looked like a long toothbrush. When the key was inserted in the hollow bolt, the fixed key pegs pushed the lock pegs up out of the holes. When the key was pulled back, it pulled the bolt with it. The door was unlocked.

The Greeks made keyholes in their doors so they could lock them from the outside. The bolt was on the inside of the door. They had a long, curved key of wood or metal that they poked through the keyhole and turned to slide the bolt.

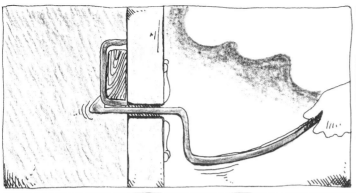

The keys had to be long enough to slide through the thickness of the door and under the bolt. Some keys were very large and hard to carry.

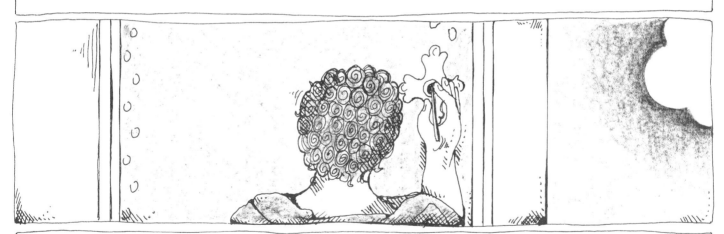

It took robbers longer to undo these locks because they couldn't see the bolts from the outside. But they tried. They twisted twigs or sharp pieces of metal through the keyhole to "pick" the lock open without a key.

About 2,000 years ago, the Romans were trying to make a better lock. They made the *ward lock*. Inside the lock was a curved piece of metal called a ward. The keyhole had notches on it. The key, too, had notches on one end. It looked like a tiny flag on a pole.

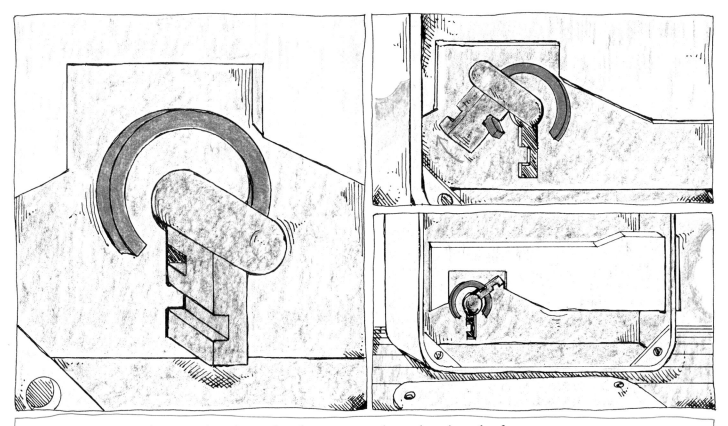

One notch on the key had to pass by the keyhole notches. Then, when the key was turned, the other notch had to slide over the ward before the key could reach the bolt to move it. Turning the key one way locked the lock; turning the other way unlocked it.

Each lock and key had its own pattern of wards and matching notches. This made it harder for a robber to open a lock. He needed the right key.

Thieves figured out they could pick even this lock with a piece of wire or a sharp, thin tool. But it took longer to do, and it was more likely that the thief would be caught. So the ward lock was the best so far.

We use ward locks today. We use them on room and closet doors, drawers, and other things. They are not as pick proof as some of our other locks, so we use them on items that are of less value to us.

But people still needed a better lock for their more important belongings. In England, about 200 years ago, the *lever-tumbler lock* was made. It was harder for a thief to pick. The key had to pass by the ward and then fit and lift a lever, called a tumbler. Then the key could move the bolt.

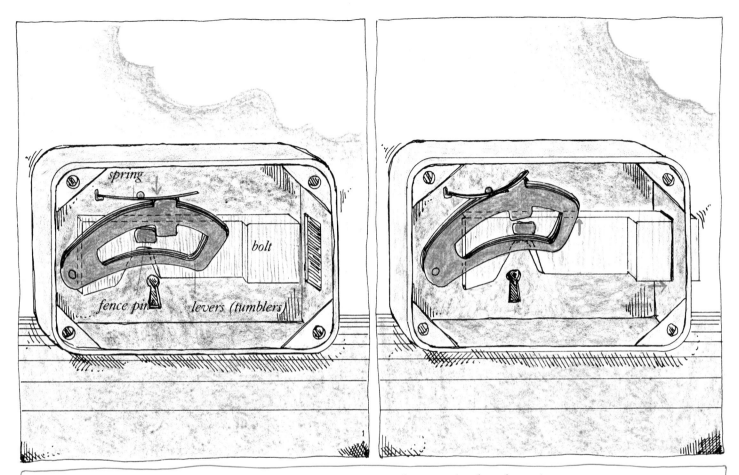

The lever-tumbler lock we use now has a bolt that is
held in place by one or more levers. The bolt has a tiny
pin, called a fence pin, on it. Above the levers, there is a
small spring. The spring pushes down on the levers.
When the levers are down, the fence pin is trapped, and
the bolt cannot move. When the levers are up, the fence
pin can pass through the opening, and the bolt slides over.

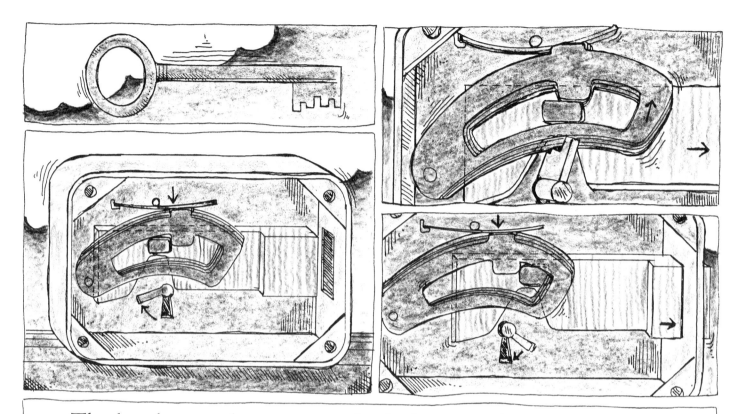

The key has notches at one end. As it turns, the notched end lifts the levers and slides the bolt at the same time. Turning the key one way slides the bolt to lock the lock. Turning the key the other way slides the bolt to unlock the lock. When the bolt has moved, the levers drop down to trap the fence pin and hold the bolt in place.

Only a key with the right pattern of notches will raise the levers so that they line up correctly to let the fence pin move. You need to have the right key for the lock.

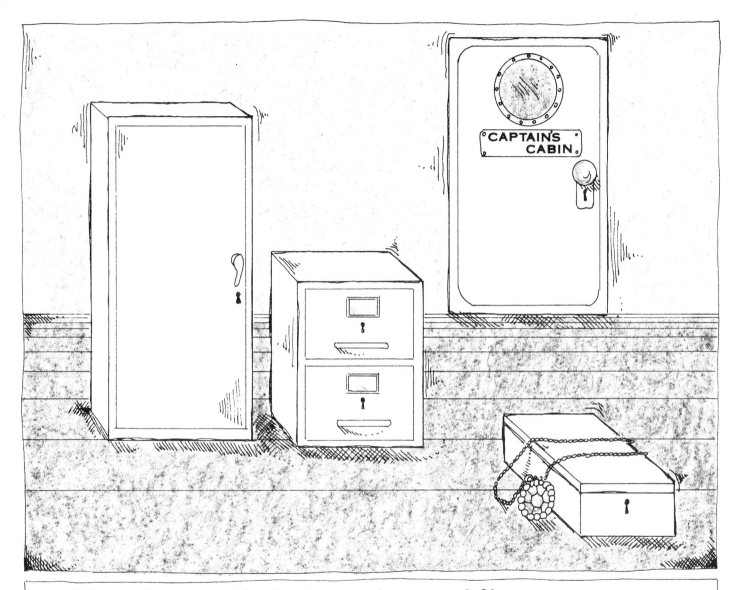

We use lever-tumbler locks on cabinets and files, on passenger doors, on bank safe-deposit boxes, and on other things that are important to lock securely.

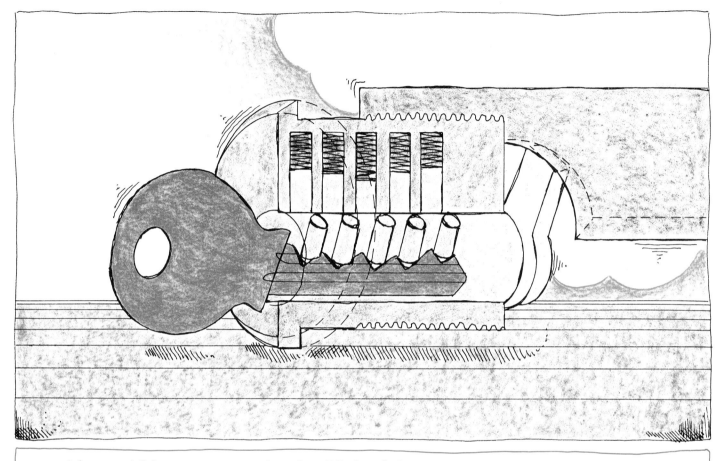

About 100 years ago, in the United States, a man
named Linus Yale invented an even better lock. This was
the *pin-tumbler cylinder lock*, or *Yale lock*. The Yale lock
was practical, too. It was the first lock that didn't need a
long key to lock or unlock it. The key didn't have to
reach far into the door to the back of the lock to move the
bolt, so only a small key was needed.

The Yale lock is similar to the old wooden Egyptian lock of 4,000 years ago. The Egyptian lock had wooden pegs that were pushed up with a key. The Yale lock, too, has tiny pegs, called pins or tumblers, that are pushed up by a key.

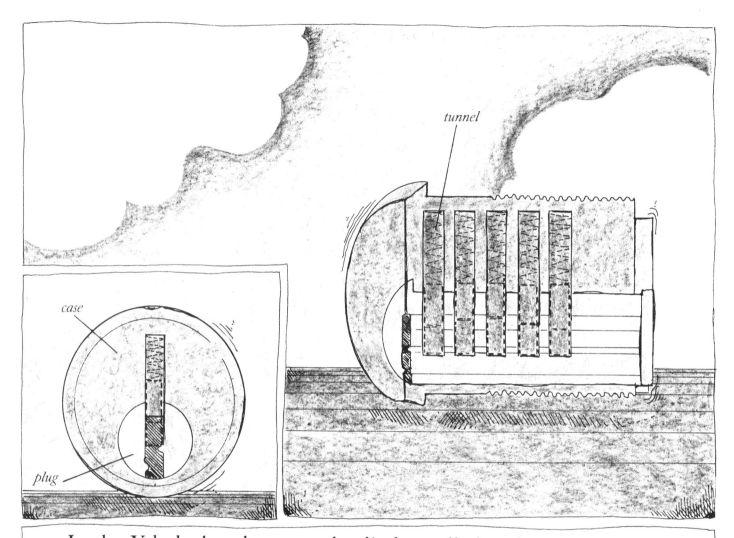

tunnel

case

plug

In the Yale lock, a long metal cylinder, called a plug, fits inside a larger cylinder, called a case. The plug has a row of tiny tunnels drilled in to it. The case has a row of tunnels, too. The tunnels in the case sit on top of the tunnels in the plug to make a row of long tunnels.

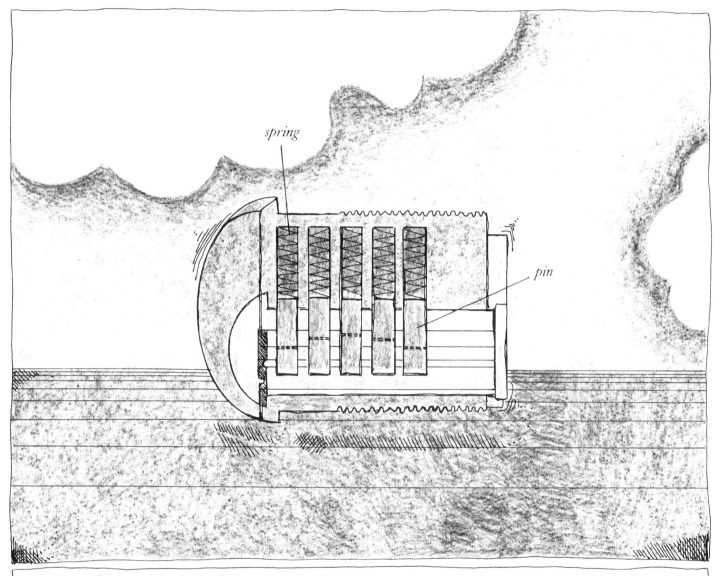

spring

pin

Inside each tunnel is a pin. Above each pin is a coiled spring. The pins sit partly in the case and partly in the plug, held firmly in place by the springs. The plug cannot turn.

Each of the pins is split into two parts, each at a different place along its length. When the key is pushed into the keyhole in the plug, it moves along under the pins and lifts them. When the key is fully in, the pins push down and fit into the notches in the key. The split in each pin now lines up with the splits in the other pins *and* with the edge of the plug. Now there is nothing holding the tunnels in the case to the tunnels in the plug. The key can now turn the plug.

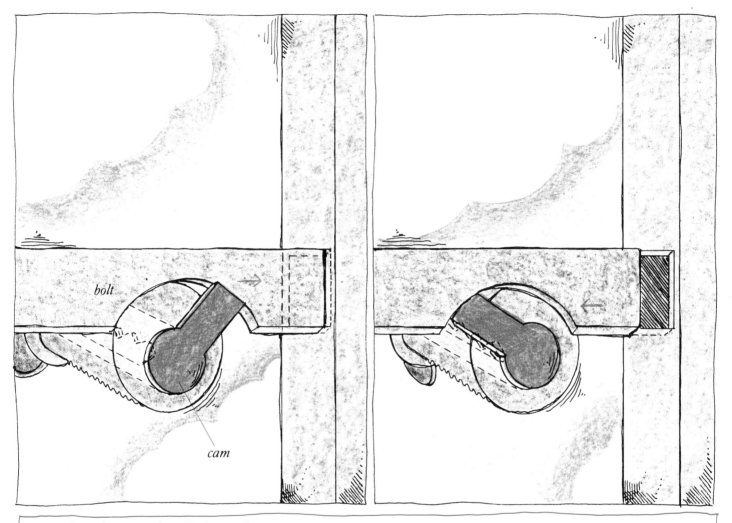

At the end of the plug is a small arm, called a cam. When the plug turns, the cam turns along with it and pushes the bolt to lock the door. When the key turns the plug the other way, the cam pushes the bolt back to unlock the door.

Only a key with the correct pattern of notches will work the lock. The pins have to be lifted just far enough so that the splits line up properly. If a wrong key is used, it may go in, but it won't be able to turn the plug.

We use the Yale lock on our front doors and other outside doors, and to lock up very important items.

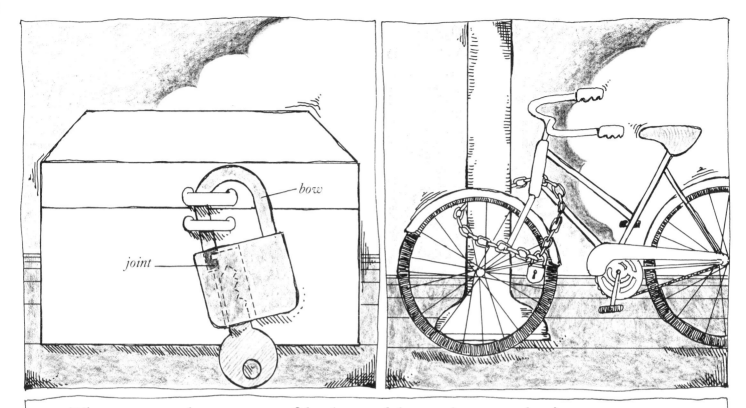

There are other types of locks and keys, but we don't use them as much as the ward lock, the lever-tumbler lock, or the Yale (pin-tumbler cylinder) lock.

The *padlock* is a portable lock. It has a rounded bow of metal that has a joint at one end. The bow of the padlock is passed through two links of a chain or through metal hasps. Then the bow is pressed down into the padlock and the joint is locked inside. To open the padlock, a key is used.

Another lock we use is the *combination lock*. It works without a key. A dial is turned to the right or to the left to line up with certain numbers that are special to that lock. Each turn of the dial moves a slotted ring into place on the inside of the lock. When the slots line up correctly, the bolt is released, and the lock clicks open.

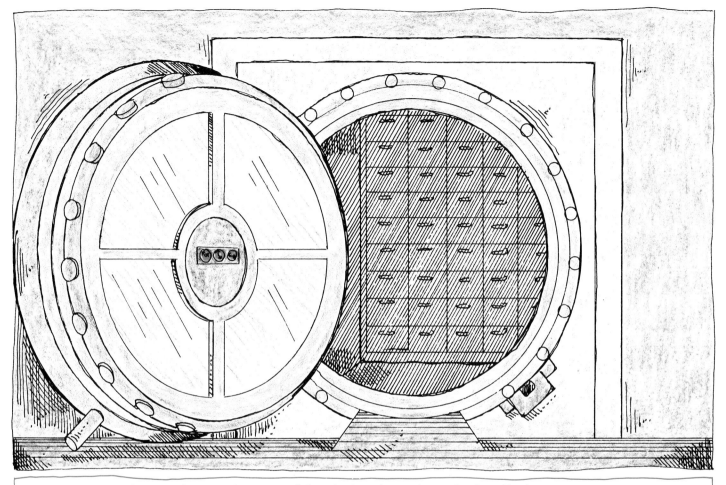

The only truly pick-proof lock is the *time lock*. It is used on bank vaults. Inside the door of the vault are a number of clocks. No one can open the door until the clocks reach the right time. When they do, a metal bar automatically slides back. Then a separate combination lock is worked to open the safe.

There are many interesting and beautiful locks and keys. Some open the doors of great castles, some open tiny boxes, and some lock up your house and my house... and open them, too.

Latches and Bolts

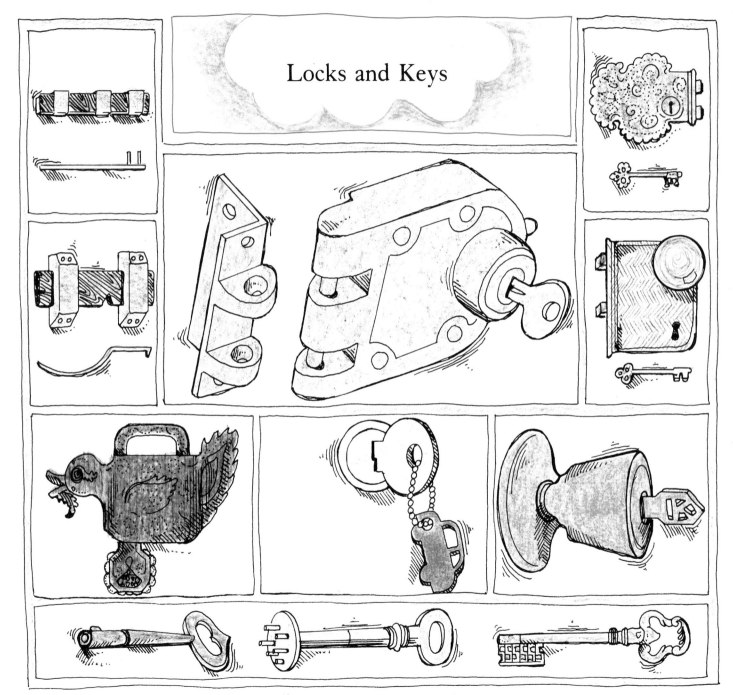

Locks and Keys